I Feel Scared

Kelly Doudna

Published by SandCastle™, an imprint of ABDO Publishing Company, 4940 Viking Drive, Edina, Minnesota 55435.

Photo credits: Adobe Image Library, Corel, Digital Stock, Digital Vision, PhotoDisc

Library of Congress Cataloging-in-Publication Data

Doudna, Kelly, 1963-
    I feel scared / Kelly Doudna.
      p. cm. -- (How do you feel?)
    Summary: In photographs and simple text, children contrast times
when they are afraid with other times when they are not.
    ISBN 1-57765-192-8
    1. Fear in children--Juvenile literature. [1. Fear.] I. Title.
   II. Series: Doudna, Kelly, 1963- How do you feel?
   BF723.F4D68 1999
   152.4'6--dc21

                                      98-27402
                                         CIP
                                         AC

The SandCastle concept, content, and reading method have been reviewed and approved by a national advisory board including literacy specialists, librarians, elementary school teachers, early childhood education professionals, and parents.

Let Us Know

After reading the book, SandCastle would like you to tell us your stories about reading. What is your favorite page? Was there something hard that you needed help with? Share the ups and downs of learning to read. We want to hear from you! To get posted on the Abdo Publishing Company Web site, send us email at:

sandcastle@abdopub.com

About SandCastle™
Nonfiction books for the beginning reader

- Basic concepts of phonics are incorporated with integrated language methods of reading instruction. Most words are short, and phrases, letter sounds, and word sounds are repeated.

- Readability is determined by the number of words in each sentence, the number of characters in each word, and word lists based on curriculum frameworks.

- Full-color photography reinforces word meanings and concepts.

- "Words I Can Read" list at the end of each book teaches basic elements of grammar, helps the reader recognize the words in the text, and builds vocabulary.

- Reading levels are indicated by the number of flags on the castle.

Look for more SandCastle books in these three reading levels:

Level 1 (one flag)	Level 2 (two flags)	Level 3 (three flags)
Grades Pre-K to K	**Grades K to 1**	**Grades 1 to 2**
5 or fewer words per page	5 to 10 words per page	10 to 15 words per page

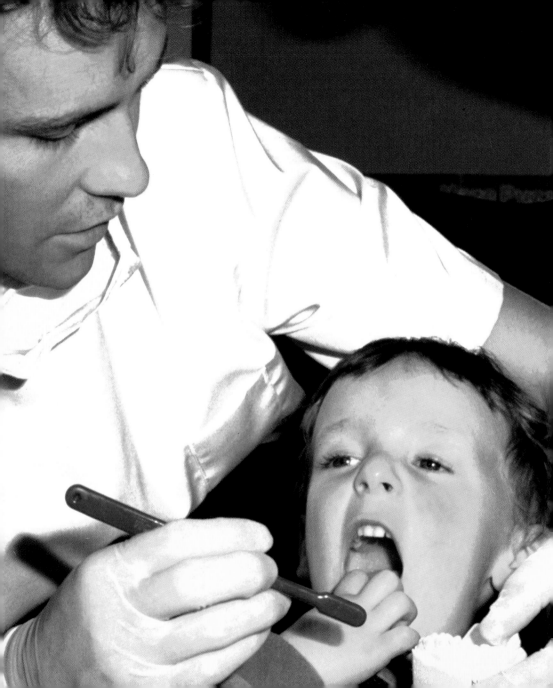

I feel scared when I must go to the dentist.

?

I am not scared when
I brush my teeth.

My toothpaste tastes like
bubble gum.

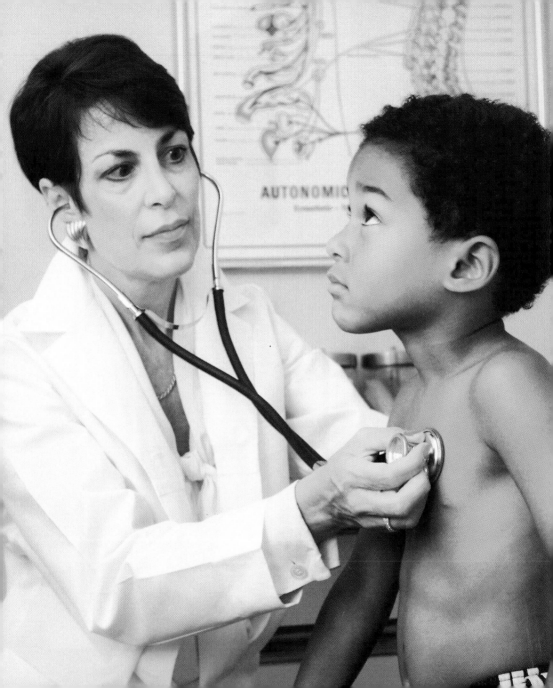

I feel scared when I must
go to the doctor.

I am not scared when Mom hugs me.

I feel better.

I feel scared when a bear
at the zoo growls at me.

I am not scared of my teddy bear.

It is soft and fluffy.

I feel scared during a storm.

Thunder is loud and lightning is bright.

I am not scared when I play in the warm sun.

It is okay for me to feel scared.

Later, I will not feel scared.

Words I Can Read

Nouns

A noun is a person, place, or thing

bear (BAIR) p. 13

bubble gum
  (BUH-buhl guhm) p. 7

dentist (DEN-tist) p. 5

doctor (DOK-tur) p. 9

lightning (LITE-ning) p. 17

Mom (MOM) p. 11

storm (STORM) p. 17

sun (SUHN) p. 19

teddy bear
  (TED-ee bair) p. 15

thunder
  (THUHN-dur) p. 17

toothpaste
  (TOOTH-payst) p. 7

zoo (ZOO) p. 13

Plural Nouns

A plural noun is more than one
person, place, or thing

teeth (TEETH) p. 7

Pronouns

A pronoun is a word that replaces a noun

I (EYE) pp. 5, 7, 9, 11, 13,
  15, 17, 19, 21

it (IT) pp. 15, 21

me (MEE) pp. 11, 13, 21

22

Verbs

An verb is an action or being word

am (AM) pp. 7, 11, 15, 19
brush (BRUHSH) p. 7
feel (FEEL) pp. 5, 9, 11, 13, 17, 21
go (GOH) pp. 5, 9
growls (GROWLZ) p. 13

hugs (HUHGZ) p. 11
is (IZ) pp. 15, 17, 21
must (MUHST) pp. 5, 9
play (PLAY) p. 19
tastes (TAYSTSS) p. 7
will (WILL) p. 21

Adjectives

An adjective describes something

better (BET-ur) p. 11
bright (BRITE) p. 17
fluffy (FLUHF-ee) p. 15
loud (LOWD) p. 17
my (MYE) pp. 7, 15

okay (oh-KAY) p. 21
scared (SKAIRD) pp. 5, 7, 9, 11, 13, 15, 17, 19, 21
soft (SAWFT) p. 15
warm (WORM) p. 19

Adverbs

An adverb tells how, when, or where something happens

later (LATE-ur) p. 21

23

Glossary

dentist - A doctor who cares for teeth.

doctor - Someone who takes care of sick people.

lightning - A flash of light in the sky during a storm.

storm - Heavy rain with thunder and lightning.

thunder - The loud noise that comes after a lightning flash.

toothpaste - A paste or gel used to clean teeth.

zoo - A place where animals live so people can see them.